Bless Your People

*Scripture and Prayers for
Parish Occasions*

Catherine H. Krier

Paulist Press
New York ♦ Mahwah

Except where indicated, scripture texts in this book are taken from the *New American Bible,* copyright © 1970 by the Confraternity of Christian Doctrine, Washington, D.C., and are used by permission of the copyright owner. All rights reserved. Excerpts from *The New Jerusalem Bible,* copyright © 1985 by Darton, Longman & Todd, Ltd., and Doubleday & Company, Inc., are reprinted by permission of the publisher.

Interior illustrations by Beverly Stoller

Copyright ©1987 by Catherine H. Krier

All rights reserved. No part of this book may be reproduced or transmitted in any form or by any means, electronic or mechanical, including photocopying, recording, or by any information storage and retrieval system without permission in writing from the publisher.

Library of Congress Cataloging-in-Publication Data

Krier, Catherine H., 1930–
    Bless your people.

    1. Benediction. 2. Catholic Church—Liturgy—Texts. I. Title.
BX2046.A1K75   1987   264′.02   87-6883
ISBN 0-8091-2890-X (pbk.)

Published by Paulist Press
997 Macarthur Boulevard
Mahwah, N.J. 07430

Printed and bound in the United States of America

Contents

◆

Introduction 3
Preface 5
Acolytes 6
Adult Choir 8
Baptism Preparation Team 10
Boy and Girl Scouts 12
Bread Bakers 14
Calendars 16
Catechists 18
Committees 21
Departure Blessings:
   College Students 23
   Families Moving Away 24
   Youth Director 26
Dismissal of a Minister of Comfort 28
Ecumenical Couples 29
Engaged Couples 31
Eucharistic Ministers 32
Fathers 34
Graduates 35
Grandparents 36
Land Mortgage Burning 37
Lectors 39
Marian Award 41
Marriage Preparation Team 42
Ministers of Hospitality 44
Mothers' Day 45
Music Coordinator 46
Musicians 48
Parish Anniversary 49
Parish Council 52
Parish Retreat 54
Parish Secretary 56
Parish Staff 58

Director of Religious Education 59
　　　Administrator 60
　　　Family Life Minister 61
　　　Liturgist 62
　　　Youth Minister 63
Pastor's Anniversary 64
Pastor's Farewell 66
Permanent Deacon 68
　　(at beginning of his formation)
Pets 69
Pilgrimage 71
RCIA Team or Director 72
Renewal of Marriage Vows 74
School Principal 76
Senior Citizens 78
Singles 79
Sponsors for Confirmation 80
Sponsors for RCIA 82
Students 84
Travelers 85
Wedding Anniversary 86
Welcome Blessings:
　　An Adopted Child 88
　　College Students 90
　　New Members 91
Widows and Widowers 92

2

Introduction

♦

Jacob blessed them, giving to each one an appropriate blessing *(Gn 49:28b).*

Come, bless Yahweh, all you who serve Yahweh. . . .
May Yahweh bless you from Zion,
the Lord who made heaven and earth
(Ps 134).

Blessings come from God, even the grace to "bless Yahweh." God is the "Giver of all gifts" and shares these gifts with us through one another. An essential component of our community prayer is remembering the blessings that God has given us. During parish gatherings we can and do invoke God's blessings upon our past, present and future lives, as well as upon the people and events that make up our lives.

By incorporating a blessing into the many and diverse parish gatherings, such as council, staff, committees and training sessions, we are able to acknowledge God's action in our lives and be open to the necessary grace to continue to live as people of faith. This provides an opportunity to single out individuals or groups who have or will have significant roles in the parish, such as the singles, widow support groups, musicians, educators. Blessings are a means of showing gratitude and support; they are a reminder of the gifts shared within the parish. Many of these gifts are hidden and need an occasional public acknowledgement. These blessings bring a personal touch to a community and help highlight the regular activities, special occasions, individuals, and families within the parish community.

This collection of blessings addresses many of the needs within the life of a typical parish. As the parishioners experience these moments of prayer they will be conscious of other celebrations that call for blessings. There is a basic structure for the blessings used in this book:

>Scripture quotation
>praise and thanksgiving to God
>request for the person/s being blessed
>in and through Christ the Lord.

Some of the blessings do not include participatory music. Music can be inserted into the above format, such as:

>sung refrain
>Scripture reading
>praise and thanksgiving to God
>request for the person/s being blessed
>in and through Christ the Lord
>sung refrain

Symbolism may also be incorporated within the blessing. Eucharistic ministers may receive a special medallion to be worn when they assume this role within the community. Bread bakers may receive a recipe and sack of flour. Catechists may be given teacher's manuals and Bibles. Musicians and choir members may be given the parish song book at their blessings.

May this book be an act of thanksgiving to God for the many members of our parishes who gather in order to serve one another in so many ways.

May the Spirit inspire you and bless you as you strive to enrich the prayer life of your parish community!

Catherine H. Krier
September 1986

Preface

♦

All you editors, bless the Lord!
All you proofreaders, bless the Lord!
All you publishers, bless the Lord!
   Praise and exalt the Lord forever!

All you friends, bless the Lord!
All you co-workers, bless the Lord!
Husband and family members, bless the Lord!
   Praise and exalt the Lord forever!

Paper and print, bless the Lord!
Pages and covers, bless the Lord!
Readers and perusers, bless the Lord!
   LET US ALL PRAISE AND EXALT THE LORD
      TOGETHER!
   AMEN! ALLELUIA!

Acolytes

♦

Certainly the role of the acolyte is less complicated today than formerly. Still, these young people need to be affirmed as much as any other ministry in the parish life. This is also a time to affirm young people within the life of the community.

To stress the dependability and prayerfulness of their role, questions or promises are asked of them prior to the blessing.

Scripture

And now what does the Lord your God ask of you? Only this:

to fear the Lord your God,
to follow the Lord's ways,
to love the Lord your God,
to serve the Lord God with all your heart
   and all your soul,
to keep the commandments and laws of the Lord
   that for your good are laid down for you.
Dt 10:12–13

Questioning

As those who have responded to God's call to the ministry of serving at the altar of God, do you stand before this assembly ready to serve? (Response)

Will you be prompt on those days that you are assigned to be an acolyte? (Response)

And do you promise to be attentive to the needs of the presider and community as we gather in prayer? (Response)

Will you respectfully pray with us while accomplishing your tasks? (Response)

Blessing

Let us pray:

Heavenly God, your Son called the children to come to him. He blessed them lovingly. We ask that you bless these your people who stand before you now. They come to serve you and this community. Grant them wisdom, age and grace as they grow in holiness, in the likeness of your Son Jesus, the Christ.

We ask this in his name and in the Spirit who calls us to serve one another. Amen.

Adult Choir

♦

In many parishes, the liturgical ministries are scheduled on a rotating basis. Yet, there is one group of ministers who appear Sunday after Sunday. And not only that, they also rehearse weekly. These ministers certainly deserve to be recognized and blessed for their dedication. The feast of St. Cecilia, the patroness of musicians, is a fitting time for this blessing.

It is also a time to restate that they are ministers within the liturgy. They are there to serve the word and the sacrament, and to assist the community's prayer. May God bless them!

Scripture

Sing gratefully to God from your hearts in psalms, hymns and inspired songs. Whatever you do, whether in speech or in action, do it in the name of the Lord Jesus. Give thanks to God the Father through him.

Col 3:16–17

Blessing

We praise you, almighty God,
    Source of all beauty.

Paul urges us to "sing to the Lord in psalms,
    hymns, and spiritual songs."
    And so we thank you for the gift of song
    in this community of faith.

We thank you for the generosity of our choir
    members.
We thank you for their time in rehearsal and in
    prayer.

We ask you to generously bless them in their efforts
    and in the fruit of their labors.
Help them as they lead us in prayer, in praise of
    you.
Bless them and their families.
Bless their director _____,
    and bless their accompanist _____.

And, finally, bless all of us as we join them in
    praise of you for ever and ever. Amen.

Baptism Preparation Team

◆

Frequently the preparation of parents for an infant's baptism is also the reintroduction of a Catholic parent to the Church. It is a time of welcoming. It may be an opportunity to welcome a new family into the local community. The team who is there to receive these young families is in a key position within the parish.

The formation and theological preparation of this team is imperative. The public acknowledgement and support of these parishioners who prepare parents for the baptism of their children is also important.

When the team is called forward for the blessing the members could carry an Easter candle, water, a baptismal garment, preparation materials and a baptismal booklet. A baptismal song or refrain could be sung as they come forward and a portion of it may be repeated after the Scripture reading.

Scripture

I want to remind you, brothers and sisters, how our ancestors were guided by a cloud above them and how they all passed through the sea. They were all baptized into Moses in this cloud and in this sea; all ate the same spiritual food and all drank the same spiritual drink, since they all drank from the spiritual rock that followed them as they went, and that rock was Christ.

I Cor 10:1–4

Blessing

God of our ancestors, Giver of faith, we gratefully praise you for our families. We beg for your blessing upon these women and men who welcome and prepare parents and children for the waters of baptism. May they be the image of Christ for all of those who come to them seeking this sacrament of initiation. We ask this of you, generous Father through Christ, Your Son and the Spirit who unites us in love. Amen.

Boy/Girl Scouts

◆

Scouts are well known for their allegiance to God and country. The scout programs help young people to build character and set goals for themselves. Respect for the earth, animals, others and self is emphasized in many ways.

This blessing is offered as a means for affirming this program as well as those who participate in it.

Psalm 91 concludes the blessing. If musicians are present they might play instrumental background music during the psalm reading. A particularly fitting selection is *On Eagle's Wings* by Michael Joncas (NALM publication).

Scripture

We pray in the name of the psalmist:
You who dwell in the shelter of the [LORD];
  who abide in the shadow of the Almighty,
Say to the LORD, "My refuge and my [strength],
  my God in whom I trust."

For he will rescue you from the snare of the fowler,
  from destroying pestilence.

With his [feathers] he will cover you,
  and under his wings you shall take refuge;
  his faithfulness is a buckler and a shield.
You shall not fear the terror of the night
  nor the arrow that flies by day;
Not the evil that roams in darkness
  nor the devastating plague at noon.

Because you have the LORD for your refuge;
  you have made the Most High your stronghold.
No evil shall befall you,
  nor shall afflication come near your tent,
For to his angels he has given command about you,
  that they guard you in all your ways.

Upon their hands they shall bear you up,
  lest you dash your foot against a stone.
"Because he clings to me, I will deliver him;
  I will set him on high because he acknowledges
    my name.
He shall call upon me, and I will answer him;
  I will deliver him and glorify him;
With length of days I will gratify him
  and will show him my salvation.

Ps 91
New American Bible

Blessing

O God of our longing, we gratefully praise you for life and health. Thank you for the opportunities to grow in knowledge and skills through the _____ Scouts of America.

May these young people fulfill their responsibilities with joyful pride by becoming good citizens of the kingdom now and forever.

We ask a special blessing for the adult leaders who dedicate countless hours to this organization and these young people. Grant them satisfaction in their work and may they receive the support and cooperation of the youth and their parents.

We ask all of this, generous God, through your Son and our Brother, and the Spirit who dwells in our hearts now and forever. Amen.

Bread Bakers

◆

There are many "hidden ministries" within our communities. The parish bulletin appears each week; linens are made and laundered.

One such ministry is that of baking bread for the Sunday liturgies. Week after week it appears, is consecrated and distributed with little or no thought to the person who prepared it.

The following blessing is composed as a token of appreciation to these people. In this instance, they are all women. However, a different wording may be chosen to include men bakers.

Scripture

A perfect woman—who can find her?
  She is far beyond the price of pearls.

She holds out her hand to the poor,
  she opens her arms to the needy.

Give her a share in what her hands have worked for,
  and let her works tell her praises at the city gates.
              Prov 31:10, 20, 31

Blessing

O God of manna, God of the one bread and one body,
  thank you for providing us with our sabbath banquet.
We praise and thank you for all of those
  who help prepare this meal week after week,
  and especially those who bake the bread
  that is consecrated at each Liturgy.
May you nourish these bakers and their families
  as you continually nourish us through this sacrament
  of your body and blood.
We ask this through Christ, the bread of life,
  for ever and ever. Amen.

JANUARY

SUNDAY	MONDAY	TUESDAY	WEDNESDAY	THURSDAY	FRIDAY	SATURDAY
				1	2	3
4	5	6	7	8	9	10
11	12	13	14	15	16	17
18	19	20	21	22	23	24
25	26	27	28	29	30	31

Calendars

♦

There are some things that happen within the life of the community that can go unnoticed. Calendars can be placed in the vestibule of the church after Christmas and people can pick them up at will. Or we can sacramentalize this as an appreciation of a New Year and a gift of time.

A simple blessing like the following can bring the "secular" into the "sacred," which is what sacramentals can do for us so well.

Scripture

There is a season for everything,
a time for every occupation under heaven:

A time for giving birth,
a time for dying;
a time for planting,
a time for uprooting what has been planted.
A time for tears,
a time for laughter;
a time for mourning,
a time for dancing.
Ecclesiastes 3:1–2, 4

Blessing

O Lord of time and eternity, Maker of the sun and the moon, we praise and thank you for the gift of time on this New Year's Day. As we begin a new year, we ask for your blessing on these calendars, reminders of the opportunities and passage of time. May we celebrate the gift of each day, remembering that it is given to us through your generous love. Help us to celebrate the significant events: birthdays, anniversaries, holidays and holydays, fasts and feasts.

   Most of all, loving God, bless each one of us who will turn these pages month by month. Be with us as we journey through the year. Through the gift of time may we come ever closer to you in health and holiness. We ask this through Christ our Lord. Amen.

Catechists

♦

How essential are the parish catechists! Their willingness to spend time in preparation and their dependability in performance are paramount to the religious education program within a community. In order to assist them in their dedication, it is important to recognize and bless them at the beginning of each school year.

In the blessing that follows the leader proclaims a Wisdom passage with dramatic expression. A suggested refrain is interspersed. This can be spoken or sung by everyone who is gathered for this blessing. During this first section the catechists may process to the place where the blessing will be given; as they process they carry lighted candles. The teachers then place the candles in an attractive arrangement around the Sacred Scriptures. The blessing is then spoken.

After the blessing teacher's manuals and the Bible may be presented to each catechist as each person is called by name.

Scripture

Refrain:
How beautiful on the mountains

are the feet of one who brings good news. (Is 52:7)

Lector:
And so I prayed, and understanding was given me;
I entreated, and the spirit of Wisdom came to me.
I esteemed her more than sceptres and thrones;
compared with her, I held riches as nothing.

Refrain:
How beautiful on the mountains
are the feet of one who brings good news.

Lector:
I reckoned no priceless stone to be her peer,
for compared with her, all gold is a pinch of sand,
and beside her silver ranks as mud.

Refrain:
How beautiful on the mountains
are the feet of one who brings good news.

Lector:
I loved her more than health or beauty,
preferred her to the light,
since her radiance never sleeps.
In her company all good things came to me,
at her hands riches not to be numbered.

Refrain:
How beautiful on the mountains
are the feet of one who brings good news.

Lector:
All these I delighted in, since Wisdom brings them,
but as yet I did not know she was their mother.
What I learned without self-interest, I pass on
    without reserve;
I do not intend to hide her riches.

Refrain:
How beautiful on the mountains
are the feet of one who brings good news.

Lector:
For she is an inexhaustible treasure . . .
and those who acquire it win God's friendship,
commended as they are . . . by the benefits of her
    teaching.

Refrain:
How beautiful on the mountains
are the feet of one who brings good news.

Lector:
May God grant me to speak as he would wish
and express thoughts worthy of his gifts,
since God is the guide of Wisdom, and directs the sages.

Refrain:
How beautiful on the mountains
are the feet of one who brings good news.

Lector:
We are indeed in God's hand, we ourselves and our words,
with all our understanding, too, and technical knowledge.
It was God who gave me true knowledge of all that is.

Wis 7:7–17a

Refrain:
How beautiful on the mountains
are the feet of one who brings good news.

Blessing

Presider: Let us pray:
Lord God, we praise you for all the gifts of the Spirit. We thank you, too, for the willingness and generosity of these catechists who stand before us. We pray that you will bless them with the wisdom and understanding, patience and perseverance to perform their responsibilities. Bless those who will come to them for instruction. May they be attentive to their words and witness of the good news of Jesus Christ. We ask this through Christ and the Spirit who live and reign with you, one God, for ever and ever. Amen.

Presentation

The presider now presents a teacher's manual to each catechist.

Committees

♦

There are so many hidden ministries that help the parish to function smoothly. The number of volunteers within the life of the parish can be most edifying. Committee members can serve for years without being recognized. The following blessing has been planned in such a way that all of these members can be recognized at the same time. Perhaps it is a joint parish council meeting or an appreciation dinner. How this is done depends upon the organization of the parish council. It can be an affirming celebration or gesture on the part of the parish staff.

Scripture

"Each one of us has been given his own share of grace, given as Christ allotted it . . . so that the saints together make a unity in the work of service, building up the Body of Christ."
Ephesians 4:7,12.

Presentations

Through our baptism we are all called to a life of service. Many people have responded to God's call to serve this community in a special way. These are the people who make up the various committees within our parish. At this time the parish council is asked to come forward. Each member of the council will present to the chairperson of the various committees a symbol of their ministry. (This list may vary according to each parish's committees.)

Buildings and Grounds	Blueprint
Family Life	Pictorial Directory
Stewardship	Checkbook
Outreach	Foodbasket
Religious Education	Teacher's Manual
Social	Plate of Cookies
Liturgy	Scripture and Stole

Blessing

Let us pray:

O Lord, from whom all blessings come in abundance, we ask for your gracious presence with these ministers. May they be blessed with wisdom, counsel and patience as they pursue the good of this community within their various areas of concern.

We ask that they be aware of our support throughout the year. May we respond to their call, as they respond to our needs. We ask all of this, Lord, in Jesus' name. Amen.

Departure of College Students

◆

Did you leave home to go off to college? Do you remember your feelings? What a step toward the unknown!

One usually has to shop around for information about the probable dates when young parishioners will begin to leave the parish for their campus life. Here is a small recognition we can offer these young men and women by anticipating their departure time.

Scripture

Whoever holds wisdom close will inherit honor, and the Lord will bless him wherever he walks.
Sir 4:12

Blessing

**Caring Lord, we praise and thank you for calling us
  to live life to its fullest.
You are the Source of all goodness, all knowledge
  and wisdom.
Bless these members of our community
  who are embarking on their pursuit of truth
  on campuses of higher education.
May they find inspiring teachers and loving friends.
May they also find a place of worship
  that will challenge them in their Christian life
  and relationship with you.
We ask this, Lord, with trust and confidence
  in your loving concern,
  through Christ our Lord. Amen.**

Families Moving Away

♦

In today's society we are a pilgrim people very much on the move, often because of employment. When a person or family has been involved in a local parish, the time of transition may be difficult for both the mover and the community.

The following blessing offers the person or family that is moving a prayerful support. It may be changed to address the parish ministry in which someone has participated. It may also include hopes and fears that they carry with them to their new city or town.

Scripture

"I am the God of your ancestors Abraham and Sarah. Do not be afraid, for I am with you."
Gen 26:24

Blessing

Ever-present God, we praise and bless you for your loving care. Bless _____ and _____ as they leave this community to return to their family in _____. This is a time of separation from their community of faith and friends. Be their Comforter during this anxious time.

We thank you for the gift that they have been to this parish. For _____, who has (here mention some way that each person has been active in the parish).

We will miss them both. May they experience our concern and prayers as they journey east to find a new home.

We ask you, Lord, to provide them with family and friends in a community of faith in _____. May their fears be turned into unexpected joys.

We ask this through Christ, your Son, and the Spirit now and for ever. Amen.

Departure of A Youth Director

♦

Parish staff members need to be welcomed into the community; so too, after their ministry is completed, they need to be affirmed and blessed as they depart from us. The following is one example of a staff blessing at the time of departure. It is a time of separation. If a youth director has been effective in his ministry it can be a difficult time for the youth of the parish. Are there ways that representative youth can be directly involved in this blessing? Perhaps a few of them can place their hands on the shoulder of the director. It is a simple gesture, yet symbolic.

Scripture

We thank our God whenever we think of you; and everytime we pray for you, we pray with joy, remembering how you have helped to spread the good news. . . .

Adaptation of Phil 1:3-4

Blessing

O ever beckoning Creator,
you who call us to the challenge of growth,
    we gratefully thank you for the gift
    that John has been to our community,
    and especially to our youth.

Although your call to _____
    to move into another area of ministry
    is a call to his growth, it is a call to separation
        from us.
We have a deep affection for him,
    and his leaving the position of Director of Youth
    in our community is a source of pain.

Bless _____ with the gifts of counsel, wisdom and
        discernment
    as he searches out a new area of employment.
May he find his new position to be a challenge
    that energizes him.
We pray that he and _____ may continue to grow
    in holiness and love.
May they be assured of lasting friendships
    and support here in our community,
        regardless of where their future may take them.
We ask this blessing, O God,
    through Christ and the Spirit. Amen.

Dismissal of A Minister of Comfort

◆

There are many aids for ministers of comfort, or ministers to the homebound. Yet, it is very important to help the worshiping community to be aware of the homebound within the parish. Certainly this can be done through the general intercessions, yet another option is to dismiss the minister just before the final blessing within the liturgy.

The eucharistic minister can take a pyx from the tabernacle just after the Communion procession. After the presider has said the Communion prayer and the announcements have been made, the Communion minister(s) can come forward for the dismissal.

Scripture

God assures us: Like a child comforted by its mother so will I comfort you.
Is 66:13

Blessing

O God, our Comforter,
  be with this minister as he (she) goes forth
  to nourish an absent member of our community
  with your word and sacrament.

May the homebound of our parish
  experience our caring support throughout this week.

We ask this of you through Christ
  and the Spirit of healing. Amen.

Ecumenical Couples

♦

Many couples are making a sincere effort to have a faith life within their homes although they worship God through different traditions. Some of these couples gather together within a parish in order to support one another's efforts and beliefs.

The following blessing may be used at one of their meetings or at some other special gathering. Everyone may sing the Alleluia response before and after Psalm 135, and repeat it between stanzas. A different member of the group proclaims each stanza. One of the leaders may offer the threefold blessing. A point must be made however: If there are non-Christian members, the threefold blessing may be offensive. It is better to omit it in this case.

Scripture

Alleluia!

**Praise the name of the LORD;
    praise, you servants of the LORD
Who stand in the house of the LORD,
    in the courts of the house of our God.**

Praise the LORD, for the LORD is good;
  sing praise to his name, which we love;
For the LORD has chosen Jacob for himself,
  Israel for his own possession.

For I know that the LORD is great;
  our LORD is greater than all gods.
All that the LORD wills he does
  in heaven and on earth,
  in the seas and in all the deeps.

He raises storm clouds from the end of the earth;
  with the lightning he makes the rain;
  he brings forth the winds from his storehouse.

And he made their land a heritage,
  the heritage of Israel his people.
Your name, O LORD, endures forever;
  LORD is your title through all generations,
For the LORD defends his people,
  and is merciful to his servants.
Blessed from Zion be the LORD,
  who dwells in Jerusalem.

Alleluia!

Ps 135
New American Bible

Blessing

May the God, whose name is kept holy in a variety of ways, bless us. Amen.

  May Jesus Christ, the risen Lord, who calls us each to follow him as individuals and as a people of God, enlighten us. Amen.

  May the Spirit, who makes us one in the beauty of our diversity, help us to love one another. Amen.

Engaged Couples

◆

Perhaps your parish has evenings for the engaged, a weekend retreat or some other occasion for gathering where a blessing may be given.

This is a significant time of transition for these couples. This is one more way for the Church to show its care and support as well as awareness of their needs.

Scripture

My dear people, let us love one another since love comes from God and everyone who loves is begotten by God and knows God. Anyone who fails to love can never have known God, because God is love. God's love for us was revealed when God sent into the world his only Son to be the sacrifice that takes our sins away. We are to love, then, because God loved us first.
1 Jn 4:7–10, 19

Blessing

O God, Source of all love and friendship, we praise you for all beauty, life and joy. Thank you for the bond of love that is present in these couples. Be with them during this time of discernment and courtship. May this be a time of fruitful dialogue for each one of them, communication both with you and with one another. We ask this, Lord, through Jesus Christ, your expression of love, who lives and reigns with you for ever and ever. Amen.

Eucharistic Ministers

◆

Some dioceses may have issued a formal mandation ceremony for eucharistic ministers. This example is an adaptation of one such mandation. When there are many eucharistic ministers they may stay in their pew and simply stand in their place during this time of questioning and blessing. Otherwise, they may be called to the front of the assembly.

Introduction

These members of our community have been through a period of training, and are now to be entrusted with administering the Eucharist not only within our liturgies, but also to the homebound and hospitalized.

I ask you, then, to be examples of Christian living in faith and conduct; may you strive to grow in holiness through this sacrament of unity and love. Remember that, though many, we are one body because we share the one bread and one cup.

As ministers of the Eucharist be, therefore, especially observant of the Lord's command to love your neighbor. For when Jesus, the Christ, gave his Body as food to his disciples, he said to them:

"This is my commandment, that you should love one another as I have loved you."

Questioning

Are you resolved to undertake the office of giving the body and blood of the Lord to your brothers and sisters, and so serve to build up the Church? I am.

Blessing

Dear friends, let us pray with confidence, asking God to bestow his blessings on our brothers and sisters, chosen to be ministers of the Eucharist:

Loving God, through the gift of the Eucharist, you have given us the sign of your love. Bless these ministers with generous love through word and sacrament. May they grow in holiness through their ministry, and may they, through their example, call us to holiness. We ask this through Christ our Lord. Amen.

Fathers

♦

Do you have a special recognition for the fathers of your parish on Father's Day? Does the community gather for breakfast after the weekend liturgies? Or do you offer coffee and doughnuts? The following blessing is another way to recognize this special role of so many men in the community.

Scripture

Honor your father and mother so that you may have a long life in the land that the Lord, your God, has given to you.
Ex 20:12

Blessing

Blessed are you, Lord and Father of all life.
You have given to us the gift of our father.
Bless him this day with your strength and holy
    power
  that he may continue to be a sign of you, our God,
  and a priestly parent to our family.
May we who have the honor of bearing his name
  do so with pride.
May we, the members of his family,
  assist him in his holy duties as a parent
    through our obedience, our respect, and our deep
    affection.
Bless him, Lord, with happiness and good health,
  with peace and with good fortune,
    so that he who shared of his very life, that we
      might live,
    may live for ever with you.

May those fathers who have preceded us in death
  enjoy everlasting life in your presence
  as they await a heavenly reunion with us.
We ask all of this, loving Parent, in union with your
  Son,
  Christ the Lord. Amen.

Graduates

◆

Although many parishes do not have elementary or high schools any longer, the parish is still able to celebrate with its graduates. The religious education coordinator or the youth director of the parish may have a special breakfast for these young parishioners. The following blessing may be offered at the same time.

Scripture

**Wisdom is bright, and does not grow dim.
By those who love her she is readily seen,
and found by those who look for her.
She herself walks about
looking for those who are worthy of her
and graciously shows herself to them as they go.**

Wis 6:12, 16

Blessing

**God of life and growth,
you have created us in your image.
We ask you to generously bless these young people
   and remain with them as a Guide in their lives.
May they always be pleasing in your sight.
May their lives be filled with every blessing.
May they be lights to the world,
   sharing your good news wherever they go.**

**We ask this through Christ and the Spirit
   who live and reign with you for ever and ever.
      Amen.**

Grandparents

♦

Within the family structure we have special people who provide a unique support for both parents and children. These are the grandparents. In some geographical areas the absence of their presence has been felt and families have "adopted" grandparents to fulfill this need. Society is recognizing their role and has now designated a special day to show appreciation for grandparents. On this day parishes could incorporate a special blessing for both natural and adopted grandparents. Children could be involved in the blessing through song and gift-giving.

Scripture

**Those who pursue virtue and kindness
shall find life and honor.**
Prov 21:21

Blessing

God of our ancestors, we bless you for the people of faith in our lives, for Abraham and Sarah, for Zechariah, Elizabeth, Joachim and Anna. We thank you too for the presence of grandparents in our lives, for their wisdom, integrity, listening ability and counsel. Bless them with peace, health and long lives.

Bless us, too, with an understanding and appreciation of their gifts and needs. We ask this of you through the Grandson of Joachim and Anna, Jesus the Lord, who lives with you and the Spirit of love, for ever and ever. Amen.

Land Mortgage Burning

♦

What a cause to celebrate! In the Hebrew Scriptures we find that the possession of land was a sign of God's blessings and covenant. Certainly parishioners can take pride in the fact that their contributions have accomplished the ownership of parish property.

Perhaps the parish will have a potluck supper or picnic in order to celebrate this event. The following blessing may also be incorporated during this gathering. A copy of the mortgage can be burned in a small hibachi. Members of the finance committee or parish council may be in a prominent position during the ceremony.

Scripture

**The land which you are to make your own
is a land of hills and valleys watered by the rain
    from heaven.
Yahweh your God takes care of this land,
the eyes of Yahweh your God are on it always,
from the year's beginning to its end.
And it is most sure that if you faithfully obey the
    commandments
I enjoin on you today,
loving Yahweh your God and serving him
with all your heart and soul,
I will give your land rain in season, autumn and
    spring rain.**
                                              Dt 11:11–14

Blessing

Because of God's gracious generosity as well as your own generous sacrifice, we are able to burn the mortgage on our land. It is with great pleasure that we will do this now with a prayer of thanksgiving:

O God of countless blessings, we praise and thank you for this gift of land that you place at our disposal. May we reverence and care for it as good and appreciative stewards. May it be a place of gathering for us where we may continue to worship you. May it be a constant sign of your blessing and covenant in our lives. And finally may we experience your Son, Christ the Lord, here on this property in the Spirit of love. Amen.

Lectors

♦

Each spring parishes may have a time and talent weekend. At this time the various ministries may be addressed and parishioners may be requested to volunteer for one of them. It is an opportunity to change ministries, leave one for a time, and for new parishioners to come forward.

After the new lectors have been through a period of training they commit themselves to their proclamation ministry. At this time they may be blessed or mandated to their proclamation of the word of the Lord.

Scripture

In full view of all the people . . . Ezra opened the book; and when he opened it all the people stood up. Then Ezra blessed the Lord, the great God; all the people raised their hands and answered, "Amen! Amen!"

Neh 8:5–6

Blessing

Praise and glory to you, Alpha and Omega,
   the Beginning and the End.
Praise to you, Eternal Word,
   who dwells with the Creator from all time.
We ask for your blessing today on these lectors
   who will proclaim your word to us.
Give them the wisdom and understanding
   necessary to inspire us
     to live your word in our lives.
May they, through their proclamation and example,
   lead us to be Gospel people.
We also ask for your blessing upon ourselves,
   so that we may hear your word
     and carry your message in our hearts.
All of this we ask of you and your word,
   Jesus the Christ, through the Holy Spirit,
     now and forever. Amen.

Marian Award

◆

Another opportunity to recognize the youth of the parish comes when young women have earned the Marian Award. These girls have been doing works of service throughout the year. This blessing is a recognition of their achievement.

Scripture

Alleluia!
Praise the Lord, my soul!
I mean to praise the Lord all my life,
I mean to sing to my God as long as I live.
Alleluia!
Ps 146:1–2

Blessing

Heavenly Lord,
I ask you to bless these medals
  as signs of the efforts and achievements
  of these young women who stand before you
    now.
May they be a reminder of their dedication to
    model
  the Mother of your Son.
May these young women continue in their
    commitment
  to "glorify the Lord"
  through their lives of service.
We ask this through Christ the Lord. Amen.

Marriage Preparation Team

♦

One of the hidden ministries within the parish community is the team that prepares couples for the sacrament of matrimony. Often the bonding that goes on between the engaged and the couples who prepare them for the sacrament continues well beyond the time of preparation. This ministry requires our support through prayer, appreciation and encouragement.

If these people have already been involved in this ministry some newly married couples who have been bonded to them through the preparation experience could be visibly involved in the blessing by standing behind them and placing their hands over the heads of team members in a gesture of blessing and/or one of them could speak the blessing.

Scripture

The kingdom of heaven is like a merchant looking for fine pearls; when he finds one of great value he goes and sells everything he owns and buys it.

Mt 13:45-46

Blessing

O God of boundless love, we bless you for the wonder of your love shown through the gift of Jesus Christ, your Son.

We ask you to bless these women and men who have generously volunteered to share their value of marriage by guiding engaged couples as they search for a life of love in union with you.

May we be available to them through our prayers and support during their time of ministry. We ask this blessing in the name of Jesus, the Lord and the Spirit who binds us together for ever and ever. Amen.

Ministers of Hospitality

♦

"First impressions are lasting"—so the saying goes. The people who are at the door to greet the strangers and regular parishioners are of primary importance.

All of us have a need to be affirmed. The ministers of hospitality (ushers) are no exception. These men and women are present to our weekend worship in a very special way. They help greet people as they arrive, see to their comfort, tend to the flow of our processions, and care for those who may be sick or have special needs during the time of community prayer.

Scripture

If someone serves me, that person must follow me; wherever I am, my servant will be there too. If anyone serves me, God will honor that person.
Jn 12:26

Blessing

Welcoming Holy One, we come with grateful hearts to worship you in your sacred temple.

Thank you for inviting us to be at home with you and one another. We gratefully acknowledge your ministers of hospitality whom you have called to serve your house of worship. May they experience the joy of serving You as they joyfully welcome us into your presence. May they be blessed with your loving care as they care for our needs. And, finally, may they, at the end of their lives, be welcomed into your holy of holies, where you live for ever and ever. Amen.

Mother's Day

♦

It is important to incorporate holidays into our Christian lives. Families usually celebrate this holiday together. Some parishes also celebrate as a family, such as the men of the parish preparing a community breakfast.

This blessing can be given while the children place their hands on their mother. This symbolizes that they bless their mother. A flower may then be offered to each woman who "mothers."

Scripture

Honor your father and mother so that you may have a long life in the land that the Lord, your God, has given to you.

Ex 20:12

Blessing

**O loving and life-giving Parent of all creation,
we praise and glorify you for life.
On this special day of recognition for motherhood,
we thank you for our mothers,
and for the gift of the co-creation of life.**

**We ask you to give them the holiness of Sarah,
Rebekah, Rachel and Leah.
May they be pleasing to you as was the young maiden,
Mary, the Mother of the Lord.**

**May they find peace and joy through union with you—
both those mothers who are living
and those who now enjoy eternal rest.**

**We ask all of this God, our Creator,
through Jesus Christ, your Son and the Spirit,
who dwells among us. Amen.**

Music Coordinator

♦

Although this collection contains blessings for the choir and musicians in general, a special blessing is offered for those parishes who have a music coordinator. This person is a resource for the parish staff, the music groups and even families who celebrate Christian burials, baptisms and other events in their lives. He or she is available for all the sacramental celebrations of the parish, such as First Eucharist, confirmation, weddings, and the Rite of Christian Initiation of Adults. The expertise is twofold: liturgy and music. Many parishioners are unaware of these gifts and the resource that the music coordinator is able to provide. A blessing is able to highlight this.

Scripture

Refrain:
Sing a new song unto the Lord,
Singing Alleluia!

Verse:
Sing Yahweh a new song!
Sing to Yahweh, all the earth!
Sing to Yahweh, bless his name.

Refrain:
Sing a new song unto the Lord,
Singing Alleluia!

Verse:
Proclaim his salvation day after day,
tell of his glory among the nations,
tell his marvels to every people.

Refrain:
Sing a new song unto the Lord,
Singing Alleluia!

Verse:
Yahweh is great, loud must be his praise,
he is to be feared beyond all gods.
Nothingness, all the gods of the nations.

Refrain:
Sing a new song unto the Lord,
Singing Alleluia!

Ps 96:1-5.

Blessing

Let us pray: O God, Creator of all sound and silence, praise and thanksgiving to you for the gift of music in our lives. Throughout sacred history this gift has enabled us to mourn, to dance, to sing and process in your presence. Bless this coordinator of music in every way but especially in _____'s ability to help us celebrate the special events in our lives, such as, weddings, anniversaries and baptisms. May he (she) assist us as we gather each weekend for Eucharist in order to express our oneness in the life, death and resurrection of Jesus Christ, your Son, through our songs of praise. We ask this through the same Christ and the Spirit of unity, for ever and ever. Amen.

Musicians

♦

This blessing is for those musicians other than the adult choir.

Again, it is important to stress their hours of preparation, expertise, and dedication. The assembly is dependent upon them as leaders in song in an essential part of our prayer life. A blessing is in order and graciously offered.

Scripture

Sing a song of praise
 blessing the Lord for all his works.
Declare the greatness of his name,
 proclaim his praise
with song and with lyre,
 and this is how you must sing his praises:
How wonderful they are, all the works of the Lord!
So now, sing with all your heart and voice
 and bless the name of the Lord!
Sir 39:14b–16, 35

Blessing

Lord of sound and silence, your gift of creation is awesome! At this time we especially bless you for your gift of music. May we never take it for granted.

 Thank you, too, for those who offer their talents as musicians during our time of worship. Thank you for their generosity of time, talent and enthusiasm. May they be blessed with renewed dedication, health and holiness.

 Bless us too, and inspire us in ways that will support them as they lead us in prayer-song. Because of their leadership and our prayerful participation may our worship be pleasing to you, Lord. We ask this in Jesus' name. Amen.

Parish Anniversary

◆

Remembering is such an important, even essential dimension of our Church life. When the anniversary of the parish community happens each year we have an opportunity to recall how God has acted in our parish history. Frequently this day comes during the summer months. It gives us an "excuse" to have a reunion with former parishioners, or even with those who have been at resorts through the summer months. Why not a parish picnic, pot luck and/or dance? Make it a festive occasion with the following blessing included.

The antiphon may be sung by everyone. The pastor and/or various parish leaders may read the Scripture quotations between the antiphon.

Scripture

"**Then Solomon said:**
'Yahweh has chosen to dwell in the thick cloud.
Yes, I have built you a dwelling,
  a place for you to live in for ever.
So now, God of Israel, let the words come true
  which you spoke to your servant David my
    father.
Yet will God really live with men and women on
  earth?
Why, the heavens and their own heavens cannot
  contain you!
How much less this house that I have built!
Listen to the prayer and entreaty of your servant,
  Yahweh my God;
Listen to the cry and to the prayer
  your servant makes to you.
Day and night let your eyes watch over this house,
  over this place in which you have promised
  to make a home for your name.
Listen to the prayer that your servants
  will offer in this place.'"
2 Chr 6:1–2, 17–20

Blessing

Presider:
Today we celebrate the _____ anniversary of our parish. This was the beginning of our family in Christ. In order to commemorate this event we would like to invoke God's blessing upon our community.

Antiphon:
Give thanks to the Lord, for the Lord is good! (Ps 138)

Leader:
Here God lives among men and women.
He will make his home among them;
they shall be his people, and he will be their God;
his name is God-with-them. (Rev 21:3b)

Antiphon:
Give thanks to the Lord . . .

Leader:
God will wipe away all tears from their eyes;
there will be no more death, and no more mourning or sadness.
The world of the past is gone. (Rev 21:4)

Antiphon:
Give thanks to the Lord . . .

Leader:
"Now I am making the whole of creation new," God said.
"Write this: that what I am saying is sure and will come true. . . .
It is already done.
I am the Alpha and the Omega, the Beginning and the End." (Rev 21:5-6)

Antiphon:
Give thanks to the Lord . . .

Leader:
But now Christ has come, as the high priest of all the blessings that were to come. He has passed through the greater, the more perfect tent, which is better than the one made by human hands because

it is not of this created order; taking with him not
the blood of goats and bull calves, but his own
blood, having won an eternal redemption for us.
(Heb 9:11–12)

Antiphon:
Give thanks to the Lord . . .

Leader:
Didn't you realize that you were God's temple
and that the Spirit of God was living in you?
If anybody should destroy the temple of God, God
   will destroy that person,
because the temple of God is sacred;
and you are that temple. (1 Cor 3:16–17)

Antiphon:
Give thanks to the Lord . . .

Presider:
Let us pray:
Emmanuel, God-with-us, we praise and thank you
for calling us to be a Christian community of faith.
Thank you too for this holy place of worship. Help
us to continue to gather in your name, to remember
the many blessings you have generously bestowed
upon _____ community. May we be a
witness to these gifts as we reach beyond ourselves
to those who do not know you or are alienated
from this community. We ask the guidance of the
Holy Spirit as we move into the future, striving to
build your kingdom now and forever. We ask this
in Jesus' name. Amen.

Parish Council

♦

Perhaps your parish is small enough to have everyone know one another. Or perhaps you utilize pictures in order to help parishioners recognize the parish leadership. One way to have parishioners see the members of the parish council is through the blessing ceremony shortly after the election has taken place.

Scripture

People must think of us as Christ's servants, stewards entrusted with the mysteries of God.
1 Cor 4:1

Questioning

As duly elected members of the parish council, I wish, first of all, to thank you for coming forward in response to the call of the Lord through the election of this community.

Do you promise to faithfully work toward the fulfillment of the goals and objectives of this community? Do you promise to faithfully strive toward the spiritual welfare of this community?

Do you promise to strive to hear and respond to the needs of the members of this community?

Blessing

We now call upon God's blessings for you and your ministry:

Blessed are you, Lord God. You have shared your
  life and grace
with this community through the willingness of
  these elected officers.

In your mercy bless them and bless their days of
  service.
May they be people of prayer and peace.
Let them live in love and service for others.

May the faith of all your saints inspire them
to follow the example of your Son Jesus,
who is Lord and Savior for ever and ever. Amen.

Parish Retreat

♦

It is time to celebrate our relationship with our God, our Friend! A parish retreat is a time when we are called *to be*—to remove ourselves from our busy schedules. It is a period of "R and R"—to simply enjoy one another, to share the Gospel of the Lord Jesus Christ, to be healed, and to have the leisure for more intense prayer. A retreat is a time for evaluation, to listen and reflect, and perhaps to set personal goals for ourselves.

This blessing can help alert parishioners to the date of the retreat and it may also address expectations on the part of the retreatants as well as the facilitators.

Scripture

There is an appointed time for everything,
   and a time for every affair under the heavens.
A time to be born, and a time to die;
   a time to plant, and a time to uproot the plant.
A time to kill, and a time to heal;
   a time to tear down, and a time to build.
A time to weep, and a time to laugh;
   a time to mourn, and a time to dance.
A time to scatter stones, and a time to gather them;
   a time to embrace, and a time to be far from
      embraces.
A time to seek, and a time to lose;
   a time to keep and a time to cast away.
A time to rend, and a time to sew;
   a time to be silent, and a time to speak.
A time to love, and a time to hate;
   a time of war, and a time of peace.
*   Eccl 3:1–8*
*   New American Bible*

Blessing

O God of the unknown, you who continually beckon us into uncharted areas, praise and thanksgiving to you. As we "retreat" from our ordinary activities we confidently rely upon your blessings. May we use this time well in order to be present to you through Sacred Scripture, through our sensitivity to one another and through our silence in your Presence. May it be a special time of grace during our spiritual journey, both as individuals and as a parish community.

   We ask this, Creator and Lord of our lives, through Jesus Christ, your Son and our Brother, and through the Spirit who teaches us how to pray for ever and ever. Amen

Parish Secretary

♦

Who is an important greeter in your community? Who is the person who frequently has the first contact with someone from outside the community? Who is a key public relations person? The parish secretary's job description is an answer to all of these questions. This task can be as varied as the people who hold the position. The following blessing focuses primarily on hospitality and communications.

Scripture

I want you to be happy, always happy in the Lord; I repeat, what I want is your happiness. Let your tolerance be evident to everyone: the Lord is very near. There is no need to worry; but if there is anything you need, pray for it, asking God for it with prayer and thanksgiving, and that peace of God, which is so much greater than we can understand, will guard your hearts and your thoughts, in Christ Jesus. Finally, fill your minds with everything that is true, everything that is noble, everything that is good and pure, everything that we love and honor, and everything that can be thought virtuous or worthy of praise . . . Then the God of peace will be with you.

Phil 4:4–9

Blessing

Hospitable and loving God, we acknowledge your graciousness in our lives. Thank you for the example of Abraham and Sarah, who welcomed the strangers into their tent. Thank you, too, for Lydia, Aquila and Priscilla, who opened their homes to Paul during his journeys. We ask your blessings on _____, our parish secretary. May he (she) reflect our spirit of hospitality to all those people who call or come to our parish office. May he (she) help to keep the channels of communication open among us, and may he (she) diligently record all that takes place in our community life so that we may remember the history of God's people in _____ parish. We ask this of you, generous Lord, through Christ, your Son, and the Spirit who makes us one. Amen.

Parish Staff

♦

The following blessings are for various staff members within a parish. By having a blessing at a public gathering, the new staff member is able to be introduced and prayed over. Prayer is not a time for education, yet indirectly the prayers do enumerate the responsibilities of the ministry. A most direct benefit is God's grace, the community's welcome and a promise of support.

Director of Religious Education

Scripture

Give ear to my words
 and apply your heart to knowing them;

For it will be a delight to keep them deep within
 you
 to have them ready on your lips.

Prov 23:17–18

Blessing

Generous Giver of all knowledge, thank You for the presence of _____ in our community.

As we entrust our children to his (her) care, we ask that you send your Spirit upon him (her).

Increase the gifts of wisdom, understanding and counsel, not only within this minister, but within each one of us.

May we support _____ in the formation of our children under his (her) leadership.

Most of all, Lord, may all of us continually help in the building of your kingdom now and in the future, until we are united with you for ever and ever. Amen.

Parish Administrator

Scripture

People must think of us as Christ's servants,
stewards entrusted with the mysteries of God.
1 Cor 4:1

Blessing

Generous and challenging Creator,
   we praise and thank you for your invitation
   to share in your life and work within creation.
We praise and thank you for the example of Jesus,
   your Son,
   who cared for the needs of people.

We ask you to bless _____ with wisdom and
   administration
   as he oversees the stewardship of this
   community.
May you support and care for him through us
   as well as his wife _____.
We ask this through Christ our Lord. Amen.

Family Life Director

Scripture

If anyone loves me he will keep my word, and my Father will love him, and we shall come to him and make our home in him.

Jn 14:23

Blessing

Holy Trinity, it is with grateful hearts that we welcome a new minister on our parish staff. _____ has graciously accepted the challenge to call us to deepen our ties as a family of faith.

May he (she) challenge our understanding of the meaning of family within the life of the home and the parish.

Grant him (her) the strength and grace to meet the demands of this position of leadership. We ask you to enable us to find the means to support _____ in his (her) ministry.

In gratitude for the gift of _____'s presence among us, we ask this blessing of you in your name, Father, Son and Spirit. Amen.

Liturgist

Scripture

One thing I ask of Yahweh, one thing I seek: to live in the house of Yahweh all the days of my life, to enjoy the sweetness of Yahweh and to consult him in his temple.

Ps 27:4

Blessing

Lord, you have called this assembly together. We come before you to give thanks and praise. We ask you to help us welcome this newest member of our staff. As a liturgist, _____ is to oversee our prayer life.

Through our support may he (she) prepare your weekly banquet through the preparation of our liturgical ministries and our place of worship.

May he (she) hear our needs and desires in giving expression to our celebration with the help of the liturgy committee.

Strengthen _____ in his (her) prayer life.

Energize his (her) creativity so that we may as a community of faith please you through our acts of worship.

We ask this of you through Christ, your beloved Son, and the Spirit who calls us to be your people for ever and ever. Amen.

Youth Minister

Scripture

At dawn and with all his heart
   he resorts to the Lord who made him;
He pleads in the presence of the Most High,
   he opens his mouth in prayer
   and makes entreaty for his sins.
If it is the will of the great Lord,
   he will be filled with the spirit of understanding,
He will shower forth words of wisdom,
   and in prayer give thanks to the Lord.
He will grow upright in purpose and learning,
   he will ponder the Lord's hidden mysteries.
He will display the instruction he has received,
   taking his pride in the law of the Lord's covenant.
                              Sir 39:5–9

Blessing

O Holy God, you who call your people to ministry, we gratefully praise you for bringing _____ into our community in order to serve the youth of this parish.

   Through his (her) teaching and example may they come to know the Lord and how to follow in his footsteps.

   May we, too, be challenged to be attentive to the needs of our young people and give us the wisdom to discern how best to support _____ in this ministry.

   We ask all of this, loving God, because of our desire to grow in holiness so that we may praise you both now and for ever. Amen.

Pastor's Anniversary

♦

This blessing could exemplify the anniversary of an ordained minister in a parish. It is an opportunity for a parish celebration, and an opportunity to affirm the priestly ministry. Priests today need to be commended and blessed for perseverance within their vocation. Here is a wonderful opportunity.

Planning committees can utilize lots of symbols at this time, such as a stole, lectionary, bread and wine, oil. Use discretion in the number.

Scripture

But, as a man dedicated to God . . . you must aim to be saintly and religious, filled with faith and love, patient and gentle. Fight the good fight of faith and win for yourself the eternal life to which you were called when you made your profession and spoke up for the truth in front of many witnesses . . . I put to you the duty of doing all that you have been told, with no faults or failures, until the Appearing of our Lord Jesus Christ.

1 Tim 6:11–12, 14

Blessing

O God of time and eternity,
you who are ever present to your people,
we praise and thank you for shepherding us.
Thank you for choosing members of your faithful
   to the ordained ministry, especially Father
   _____.

We rejoice with him on this anniversary of his
   ordination,
   gratefully acknowledging that it is a gift from
   you.

We thank you for the source of grace that this
   sacrament
   is for both Father _____ and this
   community.

Bless him with perseverance, health and
   enthusiasm in his calling.
May he experience our support as well as yours.

May we never take him for granted,
   but rather continue to grow in appreciation
   of him and his leadership.

We ask this blessing of you, Lord God,
   through Christ our Lord. Amen.

Pastor's Farewell

♦

When a pastor is transferred to another parish the community rallies around him to thank him for his ministry. During his final liturgy a symbolic litany of thanksgiving to God may be offered. This could take place at the usual time for the general intercessions or it could be after Communion.

A time for sung response is indicated. It is suggested that seven different representatives of the community offer these invocations. Each person could carry a symbolic article in procession. After the invocation the item could be given to the pastor or simply laid before the altar.

Scripture

That is why I kneel before our God from whom every family in heaven and on earth takes its name; and I pray that he will bestow on you gifts in keeping with the riches of his glory. May he strengthen you inwardly through the working of

his spirit. May Christ dwell in your heart through faith, and may charity be the root and foundation of your life. Thus you will be able to grasp fully, with all the holy ones, the breadth and length and height and depth of Christ's love, and experience this love which surpasses all knowledge, so that you may attain to the fullness of God himself.

To him whose power now at work in you can do immeasurably more than we ask or imagine—to him be glory in the Church and in Christ Jesus through all generations, world without end. Amen.
Eph 3:14–21

Presentations

Lord, in the name of all those adults and children who have been baptized into this community in the past _____ years, we thank you.
   Sung response

Lord, on behalf of the couples whose marriages have been witnessed by Father _____, we thank you.
   Sung response

Lord, Father _____ has attentively cared for the sick of the parish. Thank you for his presence.
   Sung response

In the name of those who have died, and in the name of their families, we thank you for Father's loving support.
   Sung response

Lord, we thank you for your word which has come to us through the proclamation and preaching of Father _____.
   Sung response

Lord, we thank you for the gift of the Eucharist which has been presided over by our ordained minister _____.
   Sung response

Lord, we praise you for your loving mercy. Thank you for welcoming us back into community through your servant, Father _____.
   Sung response

Permanent Deacon
At the Beginning of His Formation

◆

Parishes certainly celebrate the ordination of their permanent deacons. This is the culmination of several years of study. This blessing provides an opportunity for the community to become conscious of the period of formation. Through the blessing parishioners offer support for the candidate and his family. Hopefully, the parish can continue this support throughout the entire preparation.

Scripture

We thank Christ Jesus our Lord, who has given you strength, and who judged you faithful enough to call you into his service . . . and the grace of our Lord filled you with faith and with love that is in Christ Jesus. . . . To the eternal King, the undying, invisible and only God, be honor and glory for ever and ever. Amen.
Paraphrase 1 Tim 1:12–17.

Blessing

O God of mercy and love, we lift our voices in praise and gratitude to you. We praise you for continually calling us to new life. We thank you particularly for calling _____ to begin the formation program for the permanent diaconate. Bless him and his teachers. Give them wisdom, counsel and understanding to discern what is your will in _____'s regard, and for the good of the Church. Bless the _____ family as _____ takes on this responsibility and formation. We ask all of this, Lord, for your honor and glory through Christ our Lord. Amen.

Pets

♦

No, our dogs, cats, gerbils and rabbits do not attend our liturgies. But the liturgical connection here is the calendar of saints. Around the feast of St. Francis of Assisi (Oct. 4) children bring their pets to the parish center for a blessing. It is also a "tell and show" time. This feast also comes during the Respect for Life month. It is another opportunity for the Church to recognize the interests of children, and certainly a time for catechesis.

Scripture

All creatures great and small,	Bless the Lord.
Stars and moon,	Bless the Lord.
Sun and rain,	Bless the Lord.
Men and women,	Bless the Lord.
Girls and boys,	Bless the Lord.
Plants and animals,	Bless the Lord.
All you dogs and cats,	Bless the Lord.
All you rabbits and gerbils,	Bless the Lord.
All you snakes and mice,	Bless the Lord.
All you _____ and _____,	Bless the Lord.
All who feed and care for these pets,	Bless the Lord.
All who clean their cages,	Bless the Lord.
All who may be frightened by these animals,	Bless the Lord.

(Canticle of the Three Young Men, adapted)

Blessing

Let us pray:

Lord, Creator of life,
we praise you for the wonder of your creation.
May we always cherish the life that has been given to us.
Bless us and our pets with good health.
Help us to be responsible in our care for these creatures.
We ask this through Christ our Brother. Amen.

Pilgrimage

◆

At some time in the life of a parish a pilgrimage may take place, or "pilgrims" may request hospitality within the parish. The following blessing may be prayed at one of these times.

Scripture

Come to me, all you who are weary and find life burdensome, and I will refresh you. Take my yoke upon your shoulders and learn from me, for I am gentle and humble of heart. Your souls will find rest, for my yoke is easy and my burden light.

Mt 11:28–30.
New American Bible

Blessing

We praise and glorify you, Lord of creation, for calling all of us on the journey of life. You called Abraham and Sarah, Joseph and Mary, to travel into unknown lands. We thank you for calling these people to make a pilgrimage for your honor and glory. May their efforts be pleasing to you.

May the Lord watch over you and guide you on your journey. May his saints and angels watch over you to protect you on your way. May no harm come to you and may you reach your destination in peace and safety. And may you return safely with the Lord, who is the Source of your joy, and who is present to you always and everywhere. We ask this through Christ, who said, "Follow me." Amen.

R.C.I.A. Team
or
Director of R.C.I.A.

♦

One of the most enriching and rewarding ministries in today's Church is to be involved in the Rite of Christian Initiation of Adults. It certainly has its awesome commitment and responsibilities, yet who has been a participant in this Rite without becoming a richer person?

Some of the R.C.I.A. "alumni" could participate in the blessing with signs of the sacraments of initiation: baptism, confirmation, and the Eucharist. A musical or spoken refrain, e.g., "One Lord, one faith, one baptism" may be used throughout the blessing.

Scripture

From Simon Peter, servant and apostle of Jesus Christ: By his divine power, he has given us all the things that we need for life and for true devotion, bringing us to know God himself, who has called us by his own glory and goodness. In making these gifts, he has given us the guarantee of something

very great and wonderful to come: through them
you will be able to share the divine nature and to
escape corruption in a world that is sunk in vice.
But to attain this you will have to do your utmost
yourselves, adding goodness to the faith that you
have, understanding to your goodness, self-control
to your understanding, patience to your self-
control, true devotion to your patience, kindness
toward others to your devotion, and, to this
kindness, love. If you have a generous supply of
these, they will not leave you ineffectual or
unproductive: they will bring you to a real
knowledge of our Lord Jesus Christ.

2 Pt 1:1a, 3–8

Blessing

Refrain:
One Lord, one Faith, one Baptism.

"Alumni" 1:
May you be refreshed by the Lord as you lead others to the waters of baptism.

Refrain:
One Lord, one faith, one baptism.

"Alumni" 2:
May the Spirit counsel and guide you as you accompany others on their journey of faith.

Refrain:
One Lord, one faith, one baptism.

"Alumni" 3:
And may your own faith be nourished by the bread of life as you prepare others for full Communion within the church.

Refrain:
One Lord, one faith, one baptism.

Presider:
May the almighty God, who has gifted you with faith and the ability to share it, bless you in the name of the Creator, the Redeemer and the Sanctifier. Amen.

Renewal of Marriage Vows

◆

There are many variations of the following blessing. It can be adapted by the couple themselves, or by the family. The following example was developed by a couple on the occasion of their twenty-fifth wedding anniversary.

Just as the blessing for the anniversary of a pastor is a time of celebration and affirmation, so is this opportunity. We, as a Christian community, rejoice in the perseverance of two people whose love is centered in Christ.

Scripture

My dear people, let us love one another since love comes from God, and everyone who loves is begotten by God and knows God. Anyone who fails to love can never have known God, because God is love.

1 Jn 4:7–8

Blessing

Husband and wife:
Dear brothers and sisters in Christ,
we stand before you desiring to have you witness to our love. We continue to grow in our sacrament of matrimony. We would like you to join in this celebration of love in Christ. We pray that our marriage will be a sign and witness to God's presence in the world.

We ask for your blessing that our love will continue to grow, and that you may find a way to rededicate yourselves to the love of God through this blessing and recommitment that we speak.

Wife: It is with pride and joy that I recommit myself to you as your wife on this wedding anniversary. I desire to grow in love of you, to remain close to you for the rest of our lives.

Husband: It is with pride and joy that I recommit myself to you as your husband on this wedding anniversary. I desire to grow in love of you, to remain close to you for the rest of our lives.

School Principal

♦

A community frequently develops within a parish school. The introduction of a new school principal can be a time for this community to celebrate. The following blessing may be given during a liturgy held at the beginning of the school year. The blessing can also be offered at a school assembly or at a parent-teacher meeting.

It intentionally includes challenging goals not only for the principal, but also for the faculty, students, parents and the education department of the diocese. As the representatives speak to the principal they may offer him (her) a sign/symbol of ministry. A fitting musical refrain may be sung by the student body.

Scripture

And to some the Lord's gift was that they should be apostles; to some, prophets; to some, evangelists; to some, pastors and teachers; so that the saints together make a unity in the work of service, building up the body of Christ. In this way we are all to come to unity in our faith and in our knowledge of the Son of God, until we become the perfect body, fully mature with the fullness of Christ.

Eph 4:11–13

Blessing

Refrain:
Lord, send out your Spirit and renew the face of the earth.
Faculty Representative:
May you call us to witness the Gospel in our lives as we educate others.
Student Representative:
May you show us the value of friendship with our schoolmates and lead us to an appreciation of knowledge and truth.
Parent Representative:
May you call us to a vision of Christian family and community as well as education.
Diocesan Representative:
May you call others to see the greater needs of the Church and the world.
Refrain:
Lord, send out your Spirit and renew the face of the earth.
Presider:
May God be with you, _____, as you undertake your ministry within our community. May the risen Lord strengthen you. And may the Spirit inspire your every thought and action. Amen.

Senior Citizens

♦

There should be an occasion to recognize senior citizens within your community. The following blessing was composed for a workshop with a senior citizen group.

Scripture

How fine a thing: sound judgment with grey hairs,
  And advancing years to know how to advise!
How fine a thing: wisdom in the aged,
  And considered advice coming from men and
    women of distinction!
The crown of growing older is ripe experience,
  Its true glory, the fear of the Lord.
                                     Sir 25:5–8

Blessing

O Lord God, you who are the fullness of time,
we praise and thank you for your care and love
  throughout our journey of life.
We praise and thank you for being with us in our
    days
  of pain as well as of joy.

We ask for your blessing today;
  help us to live it fully.
May we recognize our own personal value,
  and acknowledge that we are important to others.
May we cherish today as a gift for ourselves
  and for those we will meet.

We ask this blessing with confidence,
  remembering how you have blessed us through
    our lives,
  in and through Christ, our Lord,
  and the Spirit who binds us together as sisters
    and brothers. Amen

Singles

♦

Singles are a very special group in a parish community. The witness and generosity of these people is a unique resource. It is important to be conscious of them and to respond to their needs within parish life. The following blessing is a gift that we may offer in return for their presence at our common prayer.

Scripture

The word of Yahweh was addressed to me, saying:
  Before you came to birth I consecrated you;
  I have appointed you as prophet to the nations.
  Jer 1:4–5

Blessing

Holy One, we offer you reverence, glory and praise. It is through your generous love that we receive life and its goodness. We ask for your continued generosity in the lives of the single people in our parish. May their solitude bear the fruit of close and lasting friendships. We ask too that they may continue to live lives that show concern and love for others.

Finally we ask you to grace this assembly with sensitivity toward the single people among us. Help us to welcome them into our various activities as an integral part of our family of faith. We ask all of this, O God, through Christ, your Son, and the Spirit who calls us to be your people for ever and ever. Amen.

Sponsors for Confirmation

◆

The confirmation process for our youth in today's Church has been enriched through the increased involvement of adult sponsors. A public sign of appreciation for the adult's response to this call can enrich the process of preparation.

The youth minister may call the names of the sponsor as he (she) comes forward in order to receive the blessing. As the prayer is offered the candidate for confirmation may stand behind the respective sponsor and place a hand on his (her) shoulder. After the blessing is given the sponsor may receive a manual or other book as a supportive tool and sign of responsibility and commitment.

Scripture

You are the light of the world.
A city built on a hill-top cannot be hidden.
No one lights a lamp to put it under a tub;
they put it on the lamp-stand where it shines
for everyone in the house.
In the same way your light must shine in the sight
  of all,
so, that, seeing your good works,
they may give praise to your Father in heaven.

Mt 5:14–16

Questioning

To the sponsors: On behalf of this community, I ask you:

- Are you willing to respond to the call of the Lord to undertake this responsibility? (response)
- Will you be a companion and guide to your candidate? (response)
- Will you prayerfully support the other sponsors as well as the candidates for the sacrament of confirmation? (response)

To the assembly:
And will you also include the confirmation candidates and their sponsors in your prayers? (response) Then please join me in invoking God's blessing on these sponsors:

Blessing

Let us Pray: Loving and caring God, we praise you for your presence in our lives. We thank you for your infinite mercy and kindness. We ask you to be a Source of wisdom and discernment for these men and women who stand before us now. May they journey with their candidate during this period of preparation in a way that is supportive to their companion, and at the same time may it be an opportunity for their own growth in holiness and understanding. We ask this through your Son, Jesus Christ, and the Spirit of love. Amen.

Sponsors for the R.C.I.A.

♦

To be a sponsor for someone who commits himself or herself to the initiation process is a great privilege in today's Church. It is to embark on a personal journey of renewed faith and commitment. By publicly acknowledging this event at the beginning of the process you can be a source of strength for the sponsors and, at the same time, raise an awareness of this gift and need within the parish.

Scripture

You are the light of the world. A city built on a hilltop cannot be hidden. No one lights a lamp to put it under a tub; they put it on the lamp-stand where it shines for everyone in the house. In the same way your light must shine in the sight of all, so that, seeing your good works, they may give praise to your Father in heaven.

Mt 5:14–16

Questioning

The following parishioners stand before us as Christians who have been chosen to sponsor men and women who are being initiated into the Catholic community.

On behalf of this community then, I ask you:

- Are you willing to respond to the call of the Lord to undertake this responsibility? (response)
- Will you be a friend, witness and guide to your candidate? (response)
- Will you prayerfully support the other sponsors as well as the candidates? (response)

(to the assembly)

And will you also include the participants in the Rite of Christian Initiation in your prayers? (response) Then please join me in invoking God's blessing on these sponsors:

Blessing

Let us pray: Loving and caring God, we praise you for your presence in our lives. We thank you for your infinite mercy and kindness. We ask you to be a source of wisdom and discernment for these men and women who stand before us now. May they journey with their candidate during this initiation process in a way that is supportive to their companion, and at the same time, increase their own commitment to holiness in and through you. We ask this blessing in the name of Jesus the Lord. Amen.

Students

♦

Although many parishes do not have a Catholic school, parishes are still able to recognize that children are beginning a new school year. This blessing is able to demonstrate the parish's support and care for the lives of its young people.

Scripture

Happy are the poor in spirit;
  theirs is the kingdom of heaven.
Happy are the gentle:
  they shall have the earth for their heritage.
Happy are those who hunger and thirst for what is right:
  they shall be satisfied.
Happy are the pure in heart:
  they shall see God.
Mt 5:3–4, 6, 8

Blessing

Life-giving God, we praise and thank you for your gift of life. We praise and thank you for the gift of your Son, our Brother. We ask your blessing on these young people who are beginning a new school year. May they grow in wisdom, age and grace, in the likeness of Jesus, the Lord, who lives and reigns with you, one God, for ever and ever. Amen.

Travelers

♦

Vacation time is an integral part of our lives. So often this time is spent traveling on the highways. A blessing for travelers at the outset of the summer months can show a sincere concern for one another's absence and safety. It also shows in an indirect way that members will be missed. Vacations are important, and yet, if we are a real community, we don't take a vacation from care and concern for one another. This blessing is an affirmation of times of rest and also a prayer for safe travel.

Scripture

Do not be afraid, for I have redeemed you; I have called you by name; you are mine.
$\qquad\qquad\qquad\qquad\qquad\qquad$ **Is 43:1b**

Blessing

Blessed are you, Lord of the sabbath!
Blessed are you, who rested on the seventh day!
We praise and thank you for times of rest.
We remember how you cared for your chosen people
$\quad$ **as they wandered through the desert.**
Please care now for your people who will be traveling
$\quad$ **during these summer months.**
May they travel with ease and safety.
May their vacations be a time of leisure and love,
$\quad$ **care and adventure.**
We look forward to our reunion with them when they return
$\quad$ **refreshed and with new energy.**
We ask this blessing through Christ and the Spirit of love
$\quad$ **that binds us together for ever and ever. Amen.**

Wedding Anniversaries

♦

This is another option to the renewal of marriage vows found earlier in the book. It can be a general blessing. It may be offered annually, such as around Thanksgiving Day, for any couples who are celebrating their twenty-fifth wedding anniversary within the year. At each time these couples may be given a rose.

Scripture

My dear people, let us love one another since love comes from God and everyone who loves is begotten by God and knows God. Anyone who fails to love can never have known God, because God is love.

1 Jn 4:7–8

Blessing

O God of love, _____ and _____ come before you humbly asking your blessing on their marriage.

We praise and thank you for their _____ years together. We praise and thank you for this witness of faithfulness, a witness to their children, a witness to this community.

We ask you to continue to bless their union. May their love continue to grow until they stand before you in love for all eternity.

We ask this through your Son and the Spirit for ever and ever. Amen

Welcoming an Adopted Child

◆

The following blessing addresses two needs. In today's society we frequently have the merging of multiple families through second marriages. This is a challenge for these families. The blessing addresses the need for God's help.

Secondly, some husbands and wives choose to adopt children. This blessing may be a public welcome of the child into the household; at the same time it asks for a blessing for the new parents.

Scripture

Blessed be the God and Father of our Lord Jesus Christ, who has blessed us in Christ with every spiritual blessing in heaven, even as he chose us in him before the foundation of the world, that we should be holy and blameless before him. God destined us in love to be his sons and daughters through Jesus Christ . . . to the praise of his glorious grace which he freely bestowed on us in the Beloved.

Eph 1:3-6

Blessing

Blessed be you, loving Creator of all life. Blessed be you, eternal Giver of all gifts. Blessed be you for calling this man and woman to parenting. You have given _____ the gift of natural fatherhood (motherhood). Now you call _____ to adopt this child as his (her) own through his (her) free choice.

(Parents sign the forehead of their child.)

Blessed be this child. May he (she) grow in wisdom, age and grace. May he (she) proudly bear the family name with Christian dignity.

Blessed be this mother _____. May she listen and care for _____ with the reverence of Mary. May she appreciate her maternity as did her ancestors Sarah, Hannah and Elizabeth. Grant her the graces necessary for her motherly responsibilities. May she live in faith, hope and love until her task is complete.

Blessed be this father _____. May he proudly attend to the paternal needs of this child, fulfilling his responsibilities with Christian dignity. May _____ be present to his son/daughter in the likeness of you, Yahweh, as you are toward us, your adopted children. We ask all of this loving Creator, in the name of Jesus Christ, your Son and our Brother. Amen.

Welcoming College Students Back

♦

When a young man or woman is actively involved in a dynamic campus ministry the return to the parish community in the summertime can be difficult. Even when a student has been uninvolved or minimally concerned about his or her sacramental life on a college campus, the separation from college friends during the summer months may have a need for a prayer of transition.

By offering a prayer of welcome for college students we can provide a bridge into the local church and raise our own consciousness of their presence. It can be an opportunity to ask them to be involved in liturgical ministries and other summer activities that may help them feel welcome and at home with us.

Scripture

**Rejoice in your youth, you who are young;
let your heart give you joy in your young days.
Follow the promptings of your heart
and the desires of your eyes.**

Ecclus 11:9

Blessing

Lord of our journeys, we praise and thank you for the opportunities to study and learn about the wonders of your creation. We are especially grateful today for the return of our college students. May this time with us be a period of rest, relaxation and creativity for them, a time of reunion with family and friends. We appreciate their presence among us as we praise your holy name through Jesus Christ, your Son, who lives and reigns with you and the Spirit, one God, for ever and ever. Amen.

Welcoming New Members

◆

The celebration of the sacraments of initiation is a sign of life and growth within the community. So too, is the registration of new members. A blessing may be one way of welcoming newly registered members into the community.

After the Sunday liturgy there can be a simple gathering during which time the new members may be introduced and this blessing offered. In addition the pastor and head ministers of various committees or organizations may invite them into their various groups.

Scripture

My little children . . . I give you a new commandment: love one another. Just as I have loved you, you must love one another. By this love you have for one another; everyone will know that you are my disciples.

Jn 13:33a, 34-35

Blessing

God of our journeys, thank you for your faithful presence in our lives. Thank you, too, for leading these people into our community. We ask you to bless them with the graces needed to be at home with us. Grant us the wisdom to know how to integrate them into our lives and respond to their needs. We ask this of you and your Son, whose Spirit lives in our lives now and for ever. Amen.

Widow/Widower

♦

Many parishes now have support groups for the widows and widowers. The following blessing is offered to these groups. It may be used during their meetings as new members with recent deaths join them, or it may be offered at the thirty-day anniversary of the spouse's death. This would be a means of expressing the parish's continuing support during the grieving period.

Scripture

From the depths I call to you, Yahweh.
Lord, listen to my cry for help!
Listen compassionately to my pleading!

If you never overlooked our sins, Yahweh,
Lord could anyone survive?
But you do forgive us:
   and for that we revere you.

I wait for Yahweh, my soul waits for him.
   I rely on his promise,
   my soul relies on the Lord
   more than a watchman on the coming of dawn.

Let Israel rely on Yahweh
   as much as the watchman on the dawn!
For it is with Yahweh that mercy is to be found,
and a generous redemption;
it is he who redeems Israel
   from all their sins.

Ps 130

Blessing

Comforting God, your Son Jesus experienced the death of Joseph, his father. He showed us your care for the living by breathing life into Lazarus, his friend, as well as Jairus' daughter and the widow's son. We beg you to send your strength and comfort upon these men and women gathered here in your name. May they be touched by your grace and touch one another, until the day when they are reunited with their loved ones. We ask this in the name of Jesus Christ and the Spirit-Comforter, who live and reign with you, one God, for ever and ever. Amen.

ABOUT THE AUTHOR

Catherine H. Krier serves as pastoral minister and liturgical coordinator for Christ on the Mountain Parish in Lakewood, Colorado. She has earned a Master of Music from the University of Oregon and a Master of Theology from Aquinas Institute, St. Louis. In addition to her parish ministry she is active in the Archdiocese of Denver, where she serves as Chairperson of Liturgists.